# SHARKS!

## PHONICS

# Watch That Pup

## Book 4: ch (Ending blend)

## By Quinlan B. Lee

**Photo Credits:** cover: Marc Bernardi/Alamy; title page: Doug Perrine/Getty Images; pages 2-3: Dan Callister/Alamy; pages 4-5: Marc Bernardi/Alamy; pages 6-7: ShaneGross/iStockphoto; page 8: Paul Nicklen/National Geographic; pages 10-11: Arte Sub/Alamy; page 12: Katsutoshi Ito, Nature Production/Minden Pictures; pages 14-15: Stephan Kerkhofs/Shutterstock; page16: Doug Perrine/Getty Images.

ISBN 978-0-545-74701-1

12 11 10 9 8 7 6 5 4 3 2 1          14 15 16 17 18/0

Printed in China    145

First Printing, September 2014

# SCHOLASTIC INC.

Baby sharks are called pups. Some pups grow inside their mothers.

Some pups **hatch** from eggs.

Some pups do both!

Some sharks have one pup **each** time.

Some sharks have a **bunch** of pups **each** time.

Whale sharks can have 100 pups **each** time.
That is a **bunch** of pups to **watch**!

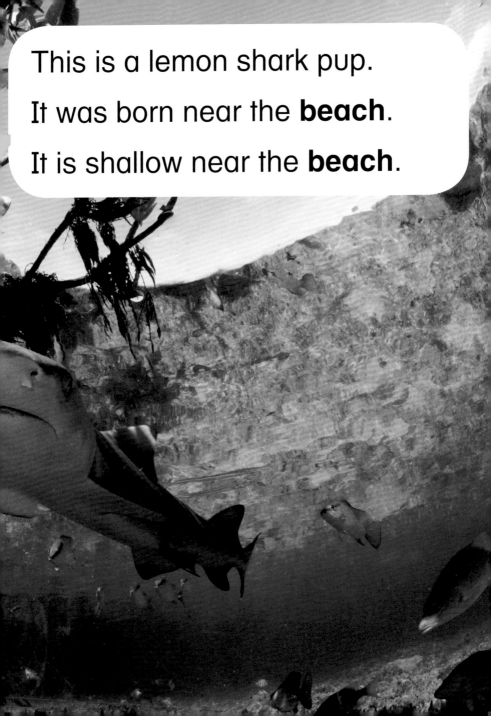

This is a lemon shark pup.

It was born near the **beach**.

It is shallow near the **beach**.

Pups stay near the **beach** so no one will **snatch** them. Sometimes other sharks like to **snatch** the pups and eat them! **Watch** out, pups!

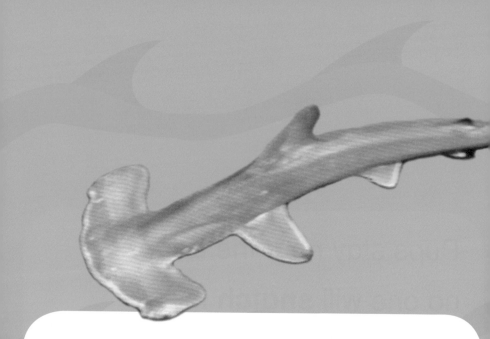

These are hammerhead shark pups.

Hammerhead pup eggs **hatch** inside their moms.

Then **each** pup grows bigger inside the mom before it is born.

Some sharks lay eggs
in the ocean.
The eggs are in a **pouch** to
keep them safe.
The **pouch** is called a
mermaid's purse.
It keeps the eggs safe until
they **hatch**.

No matter how a shark is born, it is on its own.
Its mom does not stay to **watch** it grow up.

She does not **teach** it to swim.

She does not **teach** it to hunt.

They swim away all alone.

**Watch** that pup go!